ROBERT LIMA

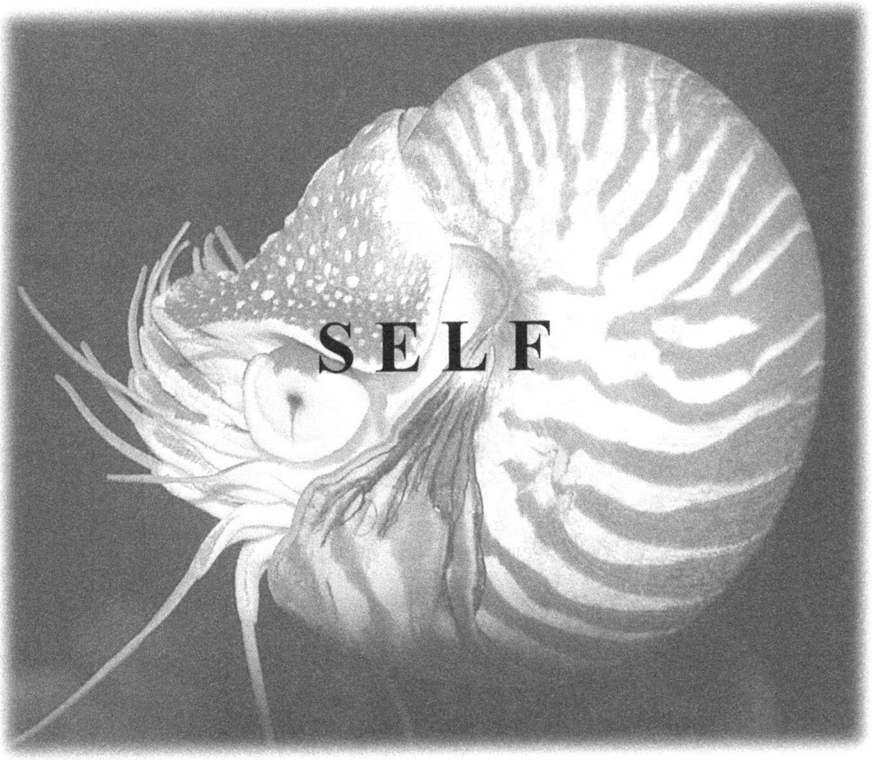

S E L F

THE ORLANDO PRESS

Copyright © 2012 by Robert Lima

All rights reserved.

No part of this book may be reproduced, stored in a retrieval system, or transmitted by any means, electronic, mechanical, photocopying, recording, or otherwise, without written permission from the author except in quotations for purposes of literary reviews by critics.

ISBN: 978-0-940804-03-6

Published and distributed by:

THE ORLANDO PRESS
485 Orlando Avenue
State College, PA 16803-3477

Acknowledgements

"I Have lost My Pity for Bones" appeared in *Town & Gown*, June 1968; in *Pivot*, 1972-73; in *Central Pennsylvania Festival of the Arts Twelve Festival Poets. 1968-1978*.

"My Heart is Deep in the Earth Roots" appeared in *Central Pennsylvania Festival of the Arts Anthology of Festival Poetry*, July 1968.

"Tracking the Minotaur" appeared in *Delta Epsilon Sigma Bulletin*, December 1970.

"Tract" appeared in *Cimarron Review*, January 1973.

"The Human Parallel" appeared in *Delta Epsilon Sigma Bulletin*, May 1973.

"Amphora" appeared in *The Literary Tabloid*, June 1975.

"Autobiography" appeared in *Sandlapper. The Magazine of South Carolina*, January, 1976.

"Peripatetic" appeared in *The Literary Review*, Winter 1980; in *Anthology of Magazine Verse and Yearbook of American Poetry*, 1981; in Spanish translation in *Liminar. Revista de Literatura y Arte*, April 1983; in *Anthology of Contemporary Latin American Literature 1960-1980*, 1986.

"Dead or Alive" appeared in *Kalliope*, Spring 1982.

"Mask" appeared in *Waterways. Poetry in the Mainstream*, May 1983.

"Demon Out of Toe" appeared in *Studies in Contemporary Satire*, Summer 1988.

"Habanera" appeared in *The Caribbean Writer*, Summer 1990; in *Pivot*, Fall 1991.

"Astrals" appeared in *Phi Kappa Phi Forum,* Spring 2009, having won the first poetry competition of the international honorary society.

The Poems

Amphora 3

As One 4

Astrals 5

Autobiography 6

Au t o n y m 7

Center 8

Cold Type: London 9

Condensation 10

Dead or Aliv e 11

Demon Out of Toe 12

Dieresis 14

Disorientation 15

Dowser 16

Habanera 17

Identity 18

I Have Lost My Pity for Bones 19

I, Nautilus 20

Mask 21

My Heart Is Deep In The Earth Roots 22

Name 23

Near Death Experience 24

Omitted ID 25

Parallel Lives 26

Peripatetic	27
Simile	28
Song for a Twilight in August	29
The Human Parallel	30
The Sea	31
Thoughts	32
Tracking The Minotaur	34
Tract	35
Window Seat	36
Writing Down the Stones	37

There are more things in heaven and earth, Horatio,
Than are dreamt of in your philosophy.
      Shakespeare, *Hamlet*

When I have fears that I may cease to be
before my pen has glean'd my teeming brain ...
      John Keats, "When I Have Fears ..."

I grow old ... I grow old.
I shall wear the bottoms of my trousers rolled.
      T.S. Eliot, "The Love Song of J. Alfred Prufrock"

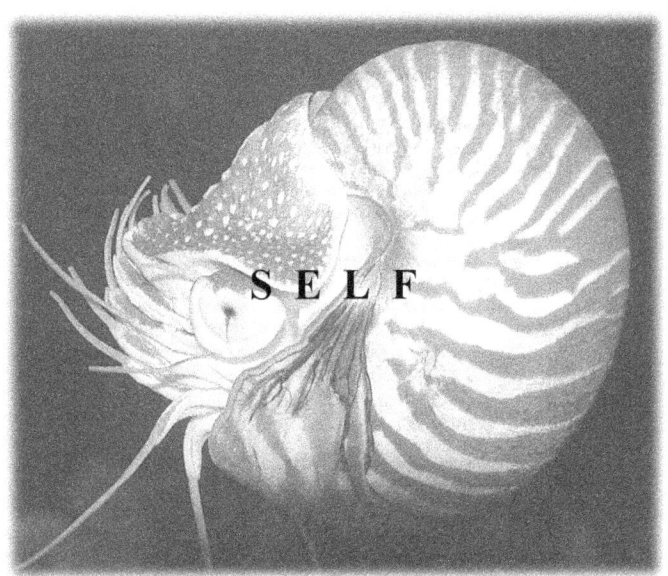

AMPHORA

The vessel that I am contains all things.
Nothing that has been is absent from my hold.

My clay façade looks individualized
(distinct, distinguishable, apart in mode),
yet I'm an old repository filled with other times.

I am totality inside this mold, everything
that has been in the times, beyond them even,
lived, suspected, known, revealed or loved . . .
all that has existed or could be . . .

Since nothing that has been somehow in time
or out, has been deprived from me, or will,
potentially all things will be in me
(or now exist, beyond the sequitur of hours).

Even when I'm dead I will be filled.

AS ONE

I face the Mountain
in its eminence, looking
at the way snow shelters
shoulders like a mantle,
at the way clouds gather
near its zenith like disciples,
at the way it faces me,
offering its pinnacle
if I would engage.

Approaching heights, my voice
is turned to snow. In turn,
the Mountain's touching wind,
its eagle's aerie call,
become an embassy to me
in answer to my inner need,
and I am filled with sight
and sound in presence of
such Mountain ways.

I am become as one,
grafting to its stone.

ASTRALS

> "We are such stuff as
> dreams are made on."
> Shakespeare

We have been taught our bodies came from dust,
to dust, then, would return at death.

Tonight, I learned that only half a truth was told
for wise astronomers, as one, now state
that stardust was the matrix ore
of which all things were ultimately made
when, primally, a Supernova burst
and sprinkled its debris across
the far-flung galaxy that's our abode.

Since then, our bodies, made of astral dust,
are longing to locate themselves once more
among the womb of stars.

AUTOBIOGRAPHY

I tire
of asking questions
that receive replies

I tire
of making the world
a better place to die

I am a Gothic man
with Baroque tendencies
dangerous to health

At all costs
keep out of reach
[if swallowed whole
induce rebirth]

AUTONYM

My name is a Portuguese river
that legions dared not cross.

My sign is a Water symbol
that stings with arachnid tail.

Born on the large Carib isla,
I've lived elsewhere at sea.

The water that has possessed me
flows inexorably through veins,
boldly sculpting contours
to shape the passage rite,
cutting chasms, mountains,
plains, in inner regions where
the definition of my self is made.

My name is a turbulent river
and my sign is bred on Water.

I need to be as Water is
for spirit to be whole in me.

CENTER

Where I am

Center,

sea's horizon

circles me,

a dot

within

the dark

confines

of night.

COLD TYPE: LONDON

It's all there--
from the hands of the typesetter
to the newsprint--
there is no room for cringing,
there's no concern for feelings:

the newspapers face me,
page one
blatant
with the fears
read in my eyes.

CONDENSATION

Inside this house
the panes of glass
bear scars

these water troughs
have sources in the air
that run on gravity
deltas in the heights
with vertical designs

I sit and watch
inside this house
as others pass
with water scars
upon their brows

      [as they see me
      in their asides]

Some rivulets are blood
and have the force
to rivet eyes
as do the scars
upon these panes of glass

DEAD OR ALIVE

Today I'm worth
what my insurance,
savings,
funds
and salary
decree.

The body's worth, what's more,
has taken an inflationary turn.

I will be worth upon my death
[with double benefits if accidentally
I leave the world of my group policy]
all but my earning power and
whatever debts have been incurred.

The statisticians measure only tangible effects.
The deficit at having left one's place
is up to the conclusion of those left behind.

The value of my bones is to be set.

DEMON OUT OF TOE

The ankle hurt like hell when it gave out on me,
the swelling mounding over bone like rising tides,
pain pounding me like waves, uneven but assured.

The healer worked upon it right away.
He took it in his hands, closed his eyes
and prayed out loud for my deliverance from pain.

His face contorted and his energy
went out of him to me in silent waves
surging over pain with faith (not mine).

He held his pendulum above the foot
and in the Savior's name tried mightily
to make the swelling go, to no avail.

He had but one recourse, he said:
to exorcise the demon in my foot, and so he did,
with ranting chants and laying on of hands.

The next day, when he asked if I had felt relief,
I lied and said I had, yet could not hide
the welling pain his touching hand evoked.

When, later on, aboard a ferry crossing Scottish seas
he tried once more, the passengers and crew
were all agog at the strange happening around my foot.

With foot in hand, he swung the pendulum again,
addressed the evil power and demanded my release at once.
And thus it came to pass, the demon left me through a toe!

My faithful healer was elated at this turn,
the vindication of his sacred craft, revealed to him alone.
And I just hobbled through without a demon in my swollen foot.

DIERESIS

I
cannot speak
to the old

I
don't know
what to say
  to bodies
  hollowed
  desiccated
  void
  vacated nearly
    apart from being

Facing them
  hypnotic stare
  abysmal
  Dies Irae eyes

I
see myself
and
cannot speak

DISORIENTATION

Sitting on the roadside . . .
there is nothing coming into view
or nearing to be heard

Nothing passes
or even distantly
allows itself
to be detected
by sight or sound

Even the usual blackbirds
have vacated the sightlines,
not even their screeches
betraying far-off presence

It is as if
the senses
had shut down
for the duration

I sit on the roadside,
eye and ear attuned,
stretching into the vacuum
waiting for sight to begin,
waiting for the silence to end

DOWSER

Sun in Scorpio, Moon in Pisces,
many Planets in the Water Signs,
I was born aboard an island
in the Caribbean Sea, whose water
still is integral to me,
as is the Celtic blood
that courses through my veins.

Born in water, borne on water
by my island craft, I seek water
everywhere I can and watch the streaks
of rain on windowpanes in search
of omens in their course on glass.

Dowser after Water for this life,
I seek to situate myself
according to its current, find
the Genius of my Place,
and fully realize the Azure Dragon
that is immanent in me.

HABANERA

I remember how the moon shone on the water
just beyond the Malecón when, as a child,
I stood against its sea wall gazing out
at gentle waves that lapped the shore
then went again unhurriedly asea to keep
a rendezvous with the horizon's stars.

Since memory cannot restore the sight itself,
my absence from that shore, where in a "once"
I played my early youth, is even greater now
that years have lapped the track of memory.

The shore recedes from mind and takes its lights,
perhaps not to be seen again, except in reveries,
the sole possession of a past that cannot be again,
the loss of moon and stars and land that once,
upon a time, were on that Caribbean Sea of mine
that now lies wanting for the want of sight.

IDENTITY

The face that stares from the mirror
does not recognize the original.

Left to right, right to left,
my semblance is amiss.

Consternation is the look
that marks each countenance.

And recognition becomes victim
to the impotence of reasoned sight.

I HAVE LOST MY PITY FOR BONES

I have lost my pity for bones
and can't kiss your dried, scarred mouth
nor visit your gravesite again.
I have neither reference nor dream
and dare not to feign at pretense
being versed in unearthing discoveries
too late in the meter of time.
Bloodshot, naive and too brave,
I have lost my pity for bones.

I have lost my pity for bones
having touched bloodless pallor death,
having kissed time oblivious to sense,
having met and uncovered this grail.
Now seeing self's reflection impaled,
I hammer and beat on the glass
and race on my wind to the place
where in the presence of Fate
I have lost my pity for bones.

I have lost my pity for bones
and shall, in the burning of tongues,
remain the adorative I
prescribing the sun to the blind,
presenting the moon to the night.
This landscape of light is humane
and sandalwood perfumes my hands
like ashes of phoenix, and yet,
I have lost my pity for bones.

I, NAUTILUS

Chambered
in concise geometry
spiraling to self
containment
propelled to depths
beyond the fathoms or
watery hypotheses
into realms of dark
capacitance
charged across the
Universe
beneath the Sea

MASK

I
My face
harbors
all
extraneously
defines
engulfs
distilling
from spirit

II
Beneath the face I wear
there are bones of passion
and of savagery that pain
bones that look out through eyes
and grasp with tensile strength

III
Possession is not only
what one holds with hands

IV
Bone eyes
devour from within
deferring only
to the outward mien

V
I have become accustomed
to this spurious face

MY HEART IS DEEP IN THE EARTH ROOTS

My heart is deep in the earth roots
chasmed in time of the ages
embedded in granite and marble
nobly enshrined in its cleavage
hard and eternal and waging
soul thoughts

forgetting
its safety from towering phases of sea
and mystical settings of clouds

until,
raging to flee to renascence
determined to settle its chaining
to rend its magnificent shrouding
and feel the lick of the sun
the grasp of the wind

it runs
diverting the earth
and
finding some moisture
proceeding to warmth

NAME

I have been designated
from my birth . . .

genetically defined
assigned identity
designed and molded
to a pattern of the time
taught to do and don't
to look beyond

until the self
imperatives have had their way
with this life's brief

a case in point
is this fey stance
a signature of ends

it is impossible to say
"I am" and be
when there is grief to cross
and names are left to be discharged

NEAR DEATH EXPERIENCE

Autoscopy

        Hovering
        in timelessness
        self-seeing
        with detachment
        of eye
        and essence

        Coming out
        of the body
        into the void
        beyond life
        as it is known

Transcendence

OMITTED ID

I choose
Not to
Enter its
Name
In the annals
Of my life.

The omission
Reverberates
Among
My readers,
Raising
Questions.

On the page,
My silence
THUNDERS

PARALLEL LIVES

To be (here),
Or not, to be (there).
That is the poser.

And thus we suffer
Through ids and egos
Of outrageous parallels
Within the universes
Of our dream-like state.

PERIPATETIC

I walk
between the cobblestones
on bricks and paving blocks

Incessantly
the steps take on the tempo
of a funereal march
through grounds deserted, wet

until
beneath the feet
papered on the footpath
I come across
the Eye of God

The God Eye
looks up my sole
and through its darkness
sees it leathery

Having overwalked
the Eye of God
without a consequence
I salivate
to tread on Death
with expert feet

SIMILE

Spiral

of extremities

Motion

emanating from the

Self

central to the core

Oneness

In / with Space

SONG FOR A TWILIGHT IN AUTUMN

I dread the sleeping on dead leaves,
on branches sprained from their limbs,
on ground unseen through its cover,
its layers of redwood, of apple and quince
possessing a terror of meaning.

Enjoying my dividend footsteps--
their hesitance, tremor and fear--
they rustle and laugh at my paleness
since subtlety never was theirs.

THE HUMAN PARALLEL

I, too, see autumn in the spring of hyacinth,
in the revelation of my red-brown hands
mixing the soil of fruitfulness
while the touching wind flatters
the ego of the cared-for flower.

In the fullness of good taste, I plan
in that eventuality
which is more,
so much more,
than the mere passing of the seasons
one upon the other's back
in the gentle motion of seducing waves.

Caressing bulbs engulf me
in their anxious patience
and as beholder I can do no more
than sit upon my hands
and wait the coming of my Spring.

THE SEA

All men are always awkward with the sea.
They handle it confusedly, with fear,
or true pretense within their arms
and cradle it bewaring its caress.

They try to feel it in their way of sense
but sea demands one's purest touch
as all its storms are clean and wild
and its embrace partakes and gives of love.

As man, I, too, am awkward with the sea
but its unspoiling kiss has touched my foot
and sent its message through me, and I say:
I have this love and I am willing to be drowned,
                                        O, Sea!

THOUGHTS

I

Thoughts
uniquely of our molding
in how we tend to them
in reverie

Thoughts
of dire acts performed,
of purpose left inactive
and the resultant ache

Thoughts
that lie upon the ragged
edges of awareness
in our torpid selves.

Thoughts
that only have connection
in vast surreal schemes
traipsing our subconscious

II

Thoughts
that spiral to extend
and then retract
into pulsations

Thoughts
like clouds on sky
returning cyclically
in déjà vu

Thoughts
that turn back on themselves
like Ouroboros seeking
to devour its tail

Thoughts
that close the circle
when the mind attains
its center

TRACKING THE MINOTAUR

We trudge to stone with listlessness
and climb the sides by clinging to inclines
that pyramid to heights with no depression.

We maze the solidarity to penetrate
and reach to core within incarceration
that trumps the mind's imagination.

We swerve avoiding the diluvian swell
and touch a depth against the soundings of our voice
that ricochet from granite breasts.

We trek in sand that sea has paralleled
and find in shells an echo of its wind
that has arisen in the desert dunes.

We wend through markers on an acute scale
and balance on a subterranean mean
that splits the vagueness into shafts.

We delve into submissiveness of thought
and preface all internment with farewells
that endings may not shatter into slivers.

We breach no barriers but the ones preset
and halt on coming to the fretted gate
that fear may have a place in heart.

We track our paths on difficult designs.

TRACT

Soon the wind will hush us dry
and all the deeds that we decry
will touch us
in our rush to stars.

I know
I'm being readied for destruction.

WINDOW SEAT

bodies
pocked by
drops of rain

random samples
designed to function
till oxidation
is completed
late
or soon

the pane
prohibits trespass
[unlike mirrors or
a looking glass]
or a warning call

I wait
redundant
in the dark

WRITING DOWN THE STONES

In a moment of moon, I am
wandering the surface of the moor
--barren, desolate and bleak--
as on a plain with an infinity
as its horizon. I am scribe
to the markers that are stones.

In a moment of moon, I am
become the age of earth itself,
ageless on its broad expanse,
limitless in warp of time
as light is halo to the lithic ring,
to dolmen, to the hallowed standing stones.

In a moment of moon, I am
t r a n s f i g u r e d
writing down the stones.

About the Author

ROBERT LIMA

is Professor Emeritus of Spanish and Comparative Literatures, as well as Fellow Emeritus of the Institute for the Arts and Humanistic Studies, at The Pennsylvania State University. He is Academician of the Academia Norteamericana de la Lengua Española and Corresponding Member of the Real Academia Española.

In 2003. he was dubbed Knight Commander in the Order of Queen Isabel of Spain by His Majesty King Juan Carlos I.

In 2011, he was presented with the festschrift *A Confluence of Words. Studies in Honor of Robert Lima*.

He is the author of twenty-eight books of poetry, criticism, biography. bibliography and translation. Over four hundred of his own poems and versions of Hispanic poems have appeared worldwide, and over one hundred-fifty of his articles have been published.

His books of poetry include *Fathoms* (1981), *The Olde Ground* (1985), *Mayaland* (1992), *Sardinia / Sardegna* (2000), *Tracking the Minotaur* (2003), *The Pointing Bone* (2008), and *The Rites of Stone* (2010).

"The Poetic World of Robert Lima: A Retrospective" was an exhibit at Penn State's Pattee Library from March through August 2004. His poem "Astrals" won the first Phi Kappa Phi poetry competition and appeared in the international society's journal *FORUM*.

He has been a Cintas Foundation Fellow in Poetry, Senior Fulbright-Hays Fellow, Commonwealth Speaker of the Pennsylvania Humanities Council, member of the Poetry Society of America, PEN, and Poets House, He is listed in *Who's Who in the World*, *Who's Who in*

America, World Who's Who of Authors and other creative writing directories in the U.S. and abroad.

http://www.personal.psu.edu/RXL2

www.ingramcontent.com/pod-product-compliance
Lightning Source LLC
Chambersburg PA
CBHW031218090426
42736CB00009B/969